SABOTAGE 2
HOW TO HANDLE A
COMMIT-A-PHOBE

IT'S ALL SMOKE AND MIRRORS

Smashwords Edition

Johanna Sparrow

SABOTAGE 2 Revised Copyright © 2016-2017 JOHANNA SPARROW

All rights reserved.
This book, or parts thereof, may not be reproduced in any form without permission from the publisher. Exceptions are made for brief excerpts used in published reviews.
www.johannasparrow.com

DEDICATION

This book is dedicated to Johanna's readers!

CONTENTS

Introduction

Resistance

Listen

Stand Your Ground

Less Is More

Give'em What They Want

Place Them on Hold

Stay Focused

Distractions

You Make the Rules

Let Them Chase You

More Red Flags

Realizing It's Over

Reinventing a New You

Talk with Johanna Sparrow

Advice from the Author

About the Author

Other Books

ACKNOWLEDGMENTS

I would like to acknowledge my friends and loved ones for helping me with this book project.

INTRODUCTION

Are you in love with a commit-a-phobe, but refusing to give up and let go? Great! Now what's next? Changing the way you think is one way you can handle a commitment phobe, since control is what is used most. Everything you do in your relationship sends a signal saying you have no problems dealing with love, but for a commitment phobe, love is scary. Commitment phobes take delight in pushing people who love them away. One minute, they're hands-off having nothing to do with you; and the next minute, they are passionate about spending time with you. Who wouldn't find this confusing? Now is not the time to lose your composure.

Commitment phobes are good at letting you in; many people may never know that they are dealing with a commitment phobe, truth be told. If you are looking to make this relationship work, you will need to meet them where they are. Commitment phobes are not going to think or act like you when it comes to love and being in a relationship, it's not going to happen. Sometimes, we want what we can't have, which is the case when dating a commit-a-phobe. Exercising patience will get you through the most difficult times in your relationship, but you must do more. Commitment phobes are not easy human beings to love because they fight you for simply loving them, crazy, isn't it? Needing a commitment phobe to validate you in a relationship only gives them the power they need to hurt you. In order to handle a commit-a-phobe, you must know where you stand and how they think, that's it. Commit-a-phobes love sending smoke signals where there is no fire and setting up trick mirrors when you aren't paying attention. To catch them at that stage, you can't believe everything they say. Did you know that the less you stress over your relationship with a commitment phobe, the more a commit-a-phobe stresses over you? It's true, and my intentions are to show you how to handle a commit-a-phobe, so you can win at love.

CHAPTER ONE
RESISTANCE

Love is not always perfect; in fact, no relationship is. But when you are in love with a commitment phobe, somehow time stands still. You can't keep going from one emotion to the next, especially if those emotions send you mixed messages. Does a commit-a-phobe understand what they are doing to you and the relationship? Yes and no. They do in the sense that they love seeing you work your butt off for them. No, because they are thinking about themselves and being hurt by love. They suck you in with sweet and kind words, somehow being the perfect everything you have been looking for. Later on, they have a change of heart when you are totally into them. Isn't that always the case? Not everyone thinks like you when it comes to relationships, but some people can love you the way you want to be loved while others, like commitment phobes, play games. Don't get me wrong, everyone wants love, it's just that some people can't or won't allow it in their lives, commitment phobes included. They want to be in a relationship, but they are afraid, so they settle for the chase and make you fall in love with them, something they have mastered.

If you are wrapped up in emotion, you will never understand a commit-a-phobe while dating them. You keep reaching for something and needing them to give it to you, wrong move. Stop cycling in and out of your mind, and get a grip on your emotions for starters. Whatever you do, never allow a commitment phobe to know that you are afraid of losing them. You will end up regretting it later on, trust me. Pull yourself together and know that being upset and angry will never give you the answers you seek or the relationship you want with a commitment phobe. It is your job to take control of your relationship since a commitment phobe does not know how. Your emotional outburst or disapproval of their behavior forces a commitment phobe to drop a disclaimer that sounds something like this, "I am afraid and have relationship issues." This is not the time to run, although you can if you want, but it is the time for you to listen closely to everything they say going forward.

What do I hear when a commitment phobe says that they have relationship issues? I hear them say, "I am afraid of love, I have been hurt when I trusted someone, please don't hurt me!" Is this real? Why is listening important? Keep reading; but for now, I guess you will have to take my word for it. You can't trust everything that comes out of a commit-a-phobe's mouth as you have learned, let them prove to you that they are truthful and ready to be in a relationship with you. As hard as that sounds, it's the only way your commit-a-phobe will show their true self, whatever that may be. Remember, they love being in control of your feelings, and when you don't allow them that, you get what you want without all of the shade and drama. Below is a list of behaviors you must adopt when dealing with a commit-a-phobe.

- You need to hold back your emotions.
- Don't tell them how you truly feel all the time.
- Learn to stay quiet.
- Challenge them on things they say.
- Never prove yourself, since it sends a message to a commit-a-phobe that you need their approval.
- Never tell them what you are really looking for such as marriage or a long-term relationship. They play games.
- Have a relaxed relationship with them that can be perceived as a friendship.
- Never bring them around the family.
- Don't assume they are in love because they let you be around their family and friends.

The key to having the relationship you want is based on what you say and do going forward. The minute you find yourself doing more is when you must pull back. You have to show resistance, or else your commit-a-phobe will expect you to yield every time. You must be responsible with the signals you send, as well as with the ones you receive. If you are tired of all of the mixed messages and games; you must make them want you. A commitment phobe has to miss you. I am sure you thought in your mind that you've done so a long time ago. Sure, you did, but that was not how that commit-a-phobe perceived it. They looked at you as the one who was desperate for love. Are they right or wrong? With each passing day, your commitment phobe does something that you don't like, and you question if you are in love with the wrong person. Right now, you care too damn much to let go, and they know that.

You will continue to feel this way unless you change the way you perceive them and the relationship you see yourself being in with them. A commitment phobe will play with your mind because they don't trust you like you trust them. Your commit-a-phobe is not comfortable in letting you in to love them, and you should know that already. It's never too late to fix what's going on in your relationship or the way your commit-a-phobe sees things. Taking time for yourself can help you regroup and understand what's happening in your relationship. Once you allow your commit-a-phobe to see you can't get enough of them, the smoke and mirrors will begin. The time you spend with them will be questioned, and your commit-a-phobe will distance him- or herself from you. The reason why commitment phobes distance themselves is that they seek to force you to want more of them. They have learned what you want, and use that against the relationship. Changing how a commitment phobe sees you sends the message you want, not the one they want to receive.

Commitment phobes watch your every move and listen to the things you say. More importantly, they pay attention to the things that aren't said, which is why you may not be experiencing the relationship that you want. Stop telling your commit-a-phobe how much you love them and that you won't hurt them, it sends them mixed messages. The more you say those things, the more fearful a commitment phobe becomes. Are you going to hurt them? Do you really love them, knowing they have not been fair with you? This is the mindset of a commitment phobe. They question everything, and trust is a major issue for them. The last message you want to send is one that says, "I am trying to prove something to you, pay attention!" News flash, that behavior alone shows guilt and tells your commit-a-phobe that you are up to something. Having a commitment phobe fall in love with you is like asking them to jump off a bridge if you know that they are afraid of heights. Did you hear what I just said?

Encouragement where there is fear only makes it worse, you must allow that person to come to you when they are ready.

No matter how loving and sweet you are, you must learn how to control yourself if you want your relationship to work. Your commit-a-phobe is afraid of you and the love you have for them. Are you going to hurt me later on? Are you going to break my heart like the last person I let in? Are you going to cheat on me? What are you going to do to me if I give my heart to you? This is the mindset of your commit-a-phobe. It's not pretty, I know, but neither is your behavior right about now, and they know this. Forcing them to love you or talk to you will cause you to lose them forever; they need to figure things out for themselves. Let them love you for being you, not because you talked a good game. They have that part down already when they play games with you.

Set limits going forward, and know that you can't rush love. You can't rush someone into getting over being afraid of love if you plan to love them no matter what. No, matter what happens in the relationship, always keep your cool and never draw attention to an area where you see your commit-a-phobe is not comfortable. Patience right now is on your side even if it does not feel that way. Below is a list of what not to do while you are setting up control and balance.

- Recognize your commit-a-phobe's signals. If they are uncomfortable about spending time, this means you must back off.

Remember, they cycle in and out when it comes to feelings and closeness.

- Try not to spend every moment with them, if you can. Remember that they are afraid of moving too fast.
- Drive the relationship and let them come to you.
- If you miss them, hold back on letting them know until they ask you.
- Keep them talking; the more they talk to you, the more you get to know what's going on inside of their head.
- Let things happen naturally. Even if you want to be intimate, don't push it. This shows a sign of control on your end.
- Learn to say no to intimacy even if you are in the mood, since many commit-a-phobes use intimacy as a way to control your emotions afterwards.

The more you want them intimately, the more emotional and mentally connected you become. Learning how to resist even the things you want sends the message, not only to them, but also to yourself, you will not allow the pleasures of love and sex to dictate your feelings or the outcome of the relationship. If you are truly ready to handle your commit-a-phobe, resistance sets the tone going forward and tells your commit-a-phobe that you have moved past the smoke and mirrors and are fully aware of what's going on.

CHAPTER TWO
LISTEN

Now that your resistance is down, I need you to focus a little bit more on your listening skills going forward. Everything you say and do is what your commit-a-phobe will use against you. Your words, behaviors and actions become their smoke and mirrors, trapping you inside your own idea of what a relationship ought to be, something they are unwilling to give to you. Instead, you find yourself proving your love and loyalty to them as if they deserve it. How much of what they've said about love and relationship have you heard? Are you only listening to yourself talking in hopes that they will fall in love with the things you have to offer? Tell me, how's that working out for you? Not good at all, but you should have been paying more attention to what your commit-a-phobe was telling you when you learned that they have issues with relationships. This is not the time to beat yourself up over the head; how would you know that your relationship was going to play out this way? In fact, you did not, and that's okay. Going forward, you will be better at knowing how to handle your commit-a-phobe, which is the focus.

Below are five keys you need to have when dealing with a commit-a-phobe.

- Listen without judging.
- Listen without feeling the need to save your commit-a-phobe from themselves.
- Listen to the things you tell them, and be prepared to not give too much of yourself away.
- Learn to trust your commit-a-phobe without defaulting them into that position because you like them.
- Allow your commit-a-phobe to prove themselves to you first.

Good listening skills are crucial to any relationship working, especially if you just so happen to have a commit-a-phobe in your life. They will tell you everything you want to hear in the beginning, and you will get caught up in the moment. That's okay, but you are past the moment and aiming towards love, if you are not already there.

Attention to detail is important and shows your commit-a-phobe that you will not be caught off guard just because they are saying all the right things you want to hear. Keeping a level head is the key when you find yourself going back and forth with your commit-a-phobe, since they may want you to show a little emotion in response to the things that they are saying even though they are not doing the same. It's okay to be happy inside when your commit-a-phobe gives in to the things you want; but don't get too comfortable in that feeling since, as you know, they love to take it back. There is nothing wrong with a little reciprocation, but keep it together.

Once again, your commit-a-phobe is trained to make you feel good and feel as if the relationship is in a good place. As soon as you show them you are happy, they will pull back and leave you an emotional wreck. The key is to make them work for your love even if you are getting what you want. A commit-a-phobe, as I said before, loves making you feel good, they love the attention of being the perfect everything you have been looking for. Don't make them everything just yet. Do you really want your commit-a-phobe to see you drooling all over them? Do you really want your commit-a-phobe to know that you can't sleep without talking to them before you go to bed? And do you want your commit-a-phobe to know how good they make you feel now that they are in your life? I hope you said no to all those questions, since a yes means your commit-a-phobe's job is done.

Sometimes, you have to use your own smoke and mirrors when dealing with a pro like a commit-a-phobe to understand what's going on. You speak too fast, and your relationship is over before you know what happened. If you don't, a commitment phobe will question whether you love them, sort of like what they may have dealt with in previous relationships. This way of thinking will allow you to see your commit-a-phobe's weaknesses, but not to hurt them; just to prevent them from hurting you. Yes, you will be using their commit-a-phobe ways against them, just not in the same way they are with you. They have told you more than you realize about how to win their hearts, if only you were paying attention. One thing is clear: Once a commitment phobe feels that they have you, they hate chasing after you. The sooner they can make you fall for them, the better and safer they feel, but you know that already. When you don't give in to your commit-a-phobe's ways, you win at controlling the relationship and indirectly force them to chase after you for the same love you seek from them, nothing's wrong with a little reverse psychology.

Let go of the fear of losing this person, or you will never have the relationship that you are looking to have with them. If you are fearful of not having them in your life, they will sense it and play around with your emotions. This is the stage where you toughen up and allow whatever happens to happen. Don't look for ways to get to spend time with your commit-a-phobe if they have not been nice to you. Let me say this, a commit-a-phobe looks for weaknesses in you that were in themselves when they got hurt, that's why running after them sends a message to not take you seriously. The last thing a commit-a-phobe wants is an image of themselves, your calling out after them only reminds them of how they acted when their heart was broken. Why on Earth would they find that behavior sexy or desirable? They simply don't, and neither should you. Nor do they want to be reminded of how foolish they acted when chasing after love with a broken heart. Does this mean your commit-a-phobe wants you to not care or give in to them? As crazy as this sounds, yes!

This assures your commit-a-phobe that you are not looking to hurt them with games and lies. They love when you are straightforward and don't chase after them. Your commit-a-phobe chooses to act like they do because it keeps them safe; remember that they once acted like you, and it cost them a broken heart. They don't want to date an old version of themselves, a fool of love, if you know what I mean. You will either toughen up or lose out – this is the mindset you must have, take it or leave it.

CHAPTER THREE
STAND YOUR GROUND

I take it you are tired of your commit-a-phobe not giving you a straight answer when it comes to where the relationship is going and whether they are on board for that ride. You are not alone. Anyone who has been through a lot and may have gotten their heart broken once or twice will have some reservations about taking those steps you want to take in the relationship. Your commit-a-phobe feels pushed into a corner; know they will come out fighting, and it won't be pretty. So, what do you do? How do you avoid having your heart and mind played with by someone who is too afraid to love you the right way? Why are you the only one in the relationship worrying? Have you gone above and beyond in making your commit-a-phobe happy? Right now, you have to stand your ground and plan how much of your heart to give away going forward.

Your relationship, unless you are careful, could end up being one-sided, and that's something you are not trying to have, trust me. Sure, you want to do things for that special person in your life, but you must caution yourself as to how they may perceive you – or your intentions, for that matter. You have a healthy way of looking at the ins and outs of what makes a great relationship, and feel that you are ready to share those experiences with that special person in your life. But not everyone is on board just yet, and you are trying frantically to win them over so that your relationship can start flourishing. You are hurting your chances by doing too much too fast, and can end up alone if you don't watch your step with your commit-a-phobe. Think about it for a moment: They are fearful for whatever reason and have gone down this road more times than they may have liked, you are not doing anything special.

Below is a list of things you can do to control your behavior if your commit-a-phobe is not responding well to your sweet gestures.

- Be less touchy-feely.
- Don't stare at them all the time. Commit-a-phobes need to feel a level of comfort just like you, and looking to engage them all the time can push them away.
- Hold back your emotions. Telling your commit-a-phobe how you missed them after spending time together is not always a good idea. It sends a message that you are becoming clingy.
- Keep your money in your pocket. Paying for dinner and a movie is a start, just try not to send the wrong message, which says "I am trying to buy your affection."

Words of love such as "I love you" or "I miss you" are not going to work on a commit-a-phobe unless these are coming from them. They will never allow you to control them when they love you.

Standing your ground simply means you are not going to lose your mind over every little thing your commit-a-phobe says or does. You are also not going to chase them, that is forbidden when handling your commit-a-phobe. The more you give them what they want or what's given in a healthy-minded relationship, the worse your commit-a-phobe is going to act out, show their ass, and become difficult for you to handle. This is the last thing you will want to experience when you have your heart exposed, trust me, and your commit-a-phobe knows this all too well. Did I mention that you will have to show a great deal of patience? That's right, because the relationship – or how you want your commit-a-phobe to behave – is not going to happen just because you love them that much. Love is the last thing on their mind; they can do without it, since it reminds them of how foolish they may have been when they fell in love.

Below is a list of attitudes and behaviors you must have when dealing with a commit-a-phobe.

- Have a fun-type mindset with them. This means that whatever happens is not a big deal.
- Don't be overly emotional. You have a

commit-a-phobe watching everything you are doing. Knowing if they have gotten to your heart is their ultimate goal. If you feel it, hold back from revealing it to your commit-a-phobe. The last thing you want to do is come across as a crazy lover.

- Set limits. This is the time to show instead of telling. Don't comment on everything they do, say or wear. It sends the wrong message: You are falling in love. That type of behavior is a turn-off for a commit-a-phobe.
- Make one comment that's positive without going into details, and move on. If you look at them, don't let them see that you are watching them.
- Make them want more or seek after your attention. When this happens, you are now in control, and your commit-a-phobe knows that their magic is not working on you like it did on others before you.
- Going out of their way will become the

commit-a-phobe's goal to win you over and have you say sweet things.
- Poker face is a must when dealing with a commit-a-phobe. Smiling simply sends a message that you are happy to be with them, not a positive thing for a commit-a-phobe to see.
- Less attention, talking and spending time is what you should focus on. You must simply do the opposite of what they are getting you to do or feel. The minute you do those things, game over or your relationship is done!

Standing your ground is keeping a level head and not making a big deal about the small stuff since your commit-a-phobe has much more proving themselves to you to do. If you are thinking you may use them by having a sort of standoffish attitude, you won't; it's the hands-on that brings these types of relationships to an end before they can get started. If your fear of losing them is bigger than your interest in protecting your heart, you will get hurt and played by a commit-a-phobe. How easy is it to have a commit-a-phobe fall in love? How long does it actually take? These questions are based on your actions, behavior and attitude. If you think that you are easy to love, then you'll see how hard it is when someone feels that is not the case. They seek for you to prove your worth to them, and all I am saying is for you to turn those tables on your commit-a-phobe. If they truly want to be in your life, they will fight for the relationship like they have for others in the past. You just have to give them a reason to fight for you, if that makes any sense at all.

Be prepared for the long haul if a commit-a-phobe is what you want. Can they love you the way you want them to? Yes, but you have to not use love to win them over. Oftentimes, people fall in love when you are not trying to love them or show them attention. This is the type of mindset you must have in your relationship going forward. Change your energy and your way of thinking, and your commit-a-phobe will feel as if they are not special enough to be in your life at this moment, then work to get that place. The harder they work, the harder your commit-a-phobe will fall in love with you; don't lose your level of cool and calmness with them.

Never go from hands-off to touchy-feely in the sense that you can't get enough of them in your life; it sends mixed messages that you are going to break their heart. Standing your ground is also about confidence that you can have anyone you want, at any given time, without needing to jump through hoops or do tricks. The higher your confidence is when it comes to dating, the more people you will attract, which says you are perfectly comfortable with being single. This is what your commit-a-phobe says to you when the tables are turned and you find yourself like a sick puppy over them. Funny how their fear and commitment issues become confidence in your face, something you were too afraid to show! When your commit-a-phobe fears losing you, they will give you the relationship that you are seeking after, now stand your ground.

CHAPTER FOUR
LESS IS MORE

You've made all of the necessary adjustments in making your relationship work, and pulling back a few things wasn't so bad. You have to keep up the good work, and know that your commit-a-phobe is looking to take back control over your emotions and feeling. This is the position your commit-a-phobe feels the safest in, don't let them get you emotional. You may have noticed them pulling away or accusing you of not loving them enough or even caring enough for them, don't fall for it! An opportunity to get you talking and sharing your feelings is what your commit-a-phobe is looking for. You have placed yourself in the greatest position, and they know this. No level of convincing them how much you care is going to relax their minds; they are looking for your weaknesses over them. *Don't give in to it, not now!*

You will feel as if you can trust your commit-a-phobe with your true feelings for them now that you see how hard they are trying to convince you that they are the real deal, but don't say a word. Anything you do to change the energy of the relationship will have you crying and in tears, back where you were before taking control and looking for answers. Remember that your commit-a-phobe has no problem with holding out on you or providing you with positive feedback to where your relationship is heading. If you need encouragement to get you going and staying on this road, consider where you were before. If you are still unsure about how to be caring when you are at the less-is-more stage, it's a good time to consider the list below.

- A wink instead of pouring out your heart allows you to show not tell them what you are feeling.
- Quick glances; nothing that shows them you are staring.
- Manners and conducting yourself in a gentlemanly or ladylike manner is the key.
- If you make eye contact when talking, avoid

deep gazing or trying to connect on an intimate level.

- If you would normally reach out to hold hands, put that off for another time. Trying to make contact is okay if you are not dating or in love with a commit-a-phobe.
- Limit how often you talk or text. Commit-a-phobes read into everything as their way of gauging where you are in the relationship. The more time you ask to spend with them, the more they know you are enjoying being in their company, and may seek to use it against you later on when they want to end things.
- If you were going out every week, put an end to it, especially if you are the one who seems to have a lot more places to go. Don't ignore it if your commit-a-phobe starts asking to see more of you. Kindly come up with something you have to do, even if you actually want to spend time with them. You must be in control of when these things

happen.
- Use social media like nothing out of the ordinary is happening, in that you are not liking everything they post. It sends the message that you are watching them, which contradicts your behavior. A commit-a-phobe knows this pattern of behavior very well, it's the one they use most often.
- Intimacy, you have to love it! No matter how bad you want them, it's a signal for you to not be intimate with them as it can put you in a more emotional state afterwards. If they are seeking to be intimate with you, keep it to foreplay, it shows how in control and in touch with yourself you are.
-

Now that you have more of an idea of how you must conduct yourself with a commit-a-phobe, it should be no problem for you to do so. It may not be easy at first, and you will feel as if you are rejecting them instead of being affectionate, but you must see what is at stake here. Love does not look good over a broken heart, I am sure you are aware of this. Once more, your commit-a-phobe will be confused and caught off guard by the change in your behavior/attitude; don't sweat, it's to be expected. Never allow them to get you into a question-and-answer session about your feelings for them, it's a set-up!

You can smile, but not every time you are with them, leave them guessing what's on your mind. I am not telling you to act angry or be mad, I just want you to look at it as if you were not out with anyone important. Friends are normally on that list because you are not trying to impress them or win them over. This is the attitude and behavior I need for you to have, since anything else will show that side of you that says: Yup, I really like you a lot! Less is more is the focus and mindset that I am trying to get you to have here. Commit-a-phobes bore easily when someone is caught up all into them and can't get enough of them. It sounds crazy since that's what a good relationship is all about, but you are not dealing with a healthy-minded person, now are you? The more you keep your feelings to yourself, the more the commitment phobe in your life will want to know how you feel about them. This is always the case no matter who you are in life. Trusting is not something a commitment phobe can do easily, and you should know this if you are heavily involved with one.

You have taken a step back in your relationship over the course of a few months to see what is really going on with the person you are madly in love with, and you are sad to see that your constant sharing of your heart has not moved them much. You still feel, for the most part, as if you are in the get-to-know-me stage of the relationship when you've done so much and should be further along. This is why I stress the importance of giving less of yourself to a commit-a-phobe, because you will not see the fruits of your devotion anytime soon. A commit-a-phobe is hard to change when they are strong in their belief that they must not get hurt when it comes to love. If you have learned anything from your relationship, it should be what your commit-a-phobe has taught you: Less is more.

You experience this side of them that you hate more often than you would like, still you pour out your beating heart in hopes that they will let down their guard and welcome you into their world. Not going to happen, it's not that easy, and what you will then want more than anything must be you not falling apart or giving in when you are not treated the way you feel you should. Those are the rules. I did not make them up, but your commit-a-phobe did. And whether you like it or not, you have been following, that much they know.

Give yourself credit for sticking things out this long, someone else would have called it quits a long time ago. The only way you are going to have any control over having your heart stepped on by that commitment phobe in your life is by not allowing them to win you over so fast. The quicker they can be your everything, the sooner they are on their way out the door, it's just that simple.

Every time you give a little more or say a little

more about your feelings to them, you may find that they are not as interested as they work so hard for you to become. In fact, loving you should not be that easy, and your worth should be something the other person needs to work for if they want to get or stay in a good place with you. You may get the idea that you are going to secure the relationship or give them some warm and fuzzy feeling about you deep down inside simply by telling your commit-a-phobe that they are everything you need and by asking why they aren't pouring out their heart in the same way. If you actually believe that, then you need more help than I thought. It's like your favorite sport: What happens when you've built up the hype, attended the game, and had the time of your life is that the fun is soon over with your team winning, and such is the case in the relationship. Let's just say that you showed up to play, and the commit-a-phobe put on a great show; now you are out of your mind crazy in love with them, and they just don't understand why.

Hello, weren't they the one putting on the charm

or getting you so hot that you both could not keep your hands off of each other? It's enough to wonder if you were misled in your emotions, and the answer is yes and no. A commit-a-phobe is not going to put forth effort in someone if they don't like them at first, not going to happen. Since you are experiencing this, it means that they were and still are into you, it's just that you made all of the serious moves toward them while they were... sort of testing the waters, I should say. Secondly, you made it easy for them. I mean you bought into everything they told you, not to mention things you may have added along the way. When falling for a commit-a-phobe, the only person who should know what's going on is you. Let's just say your commit-a-phobe is not mentally prepared to hear all of the wonderful things you think of them without having a panic or anxiety attack. Your smooth loving and confident moves send them running for the hills and fast; I mean, the last thing they want is for you to take them seriously. There is nothing wrong with confidence in a relationship with a healthy-minded individual; but with a commit-a-phobe, you are asking for a roller coaster ride that you may have a difficult time getting off.

    Raise your confidence level enough to hold back your emotions, allowing your commit-a-phobe to win you over while never ever getting that satisfaction, because you keep them reaching while only giving them a little bit of you when you want and not when they feel they should have it.

CHAPTER FIVE
GIVE'EM WHAT THEY WANT

You have had your fair share of ups and downs in what seems to be a wacky and out-of-touch relationship. Your commitment phobe seems to think he/she knows what sets you off, and they are right. You hate it when one minute, they are all into you, and the next they are not sure if they know you. This mental cycling a commit-a-phobe does can drive the sanest person out of their minds, literally. You have been trying to track their behavior on your own, and it's not working. They have burned you out of love, no one is talking, and you need the break.

This is the fifth time in your relationship that they have taken a backseat in helping the relationship go to the next level. Now you are tired, and you should be. You've given your heart and soul to make this crazy relationship work. Heck, if it wasn't for you, they would not have anyone in their life, this is for damn sure. Why are you taking this? Why are you giving in to them and crying when they hurt you? Is it love that has you so dumbfounded over what's really going on? The relationship is drowning, and they are too freaking heartless to help save what you both have built.

Face it, you knew that they were hot and cold when it came to your relationship. In fact, they have been playing around with your emotions for some time. Get a grip on yourself, it's time you pull back. You've given in way too much, and they have control. The more control a commit-a-phobe has, the less you will get what you want, namely love. Stop being afraid of being alone; if this is the best you can do, cut your losses. If you are in love, you must outsmart your commit-a-phobe. They love playing with your heart. It's not going to stop until you put your foot down. They are not going to miss you or want you until you put your foot down. Heck, they are not going to see you or your worth until, you guess what, you put your foot down.

Below is a list of things you need to avoid in order to put your foot down in the relationship.

- Running over to or making time for your commit-a-phobe when they aren't making time for you.
- Taking their call or texting them every time as if you have an infinite amount of time to respond.
- Telling them everything that's going on in your life, like how you have no one but them.
- Getting upset when they disappoint you or stand you up.
- Begging to be intimate with them.
- Going out of your way to make them comfortable even when they don't deserve it.
- Not giving them the space they need, back off.

Now that you see what you need to avoid doing to put down your foot on, stop doing those things. There is nothing that says "I am weak" more than doing everything your commit-a-phobe asks of you. News flash: You don't need them, and it's time you show them that. Hell, they should be lucky to have you in their life. This is the part where you should know your worth and stop playing into the hands of someone who's clueless when it comes to relationships and love.

It's high time that you give your commit-a-phobe exactly what he/she has been asking for. One of two things will happen when you stand your ground and protect yourself in this type of relationship.

You will gain respect and feel better.

You will reconsider your relationship.

It's your responsibility to get what you want from the relationship. If you are not happy, you must re-evaluate your partner's position. The worst you can do while dating a commit-a-phobe is give in to everything they say while chasing after them. *Commit-a-phobes don't think highly of you when you act this way, so stop it!*

Stop making things harder than they already are,

you deserve the best, make them give it to you. Everyone has a side of themselves that can be taken, you just need to know how to get to it. Stop begging for your commit-a-phobe to spend time with you, and keep busy. *The more you go about life, the more they will want to share your world with you.*

CHAPTER SIX
PLACE THEM ON HOLD

No one likes being put on hold, not even a commitment phobe, but it's what they need from time to time. Taking charge does not always mean raising your voice or stating facts; nope, just placing someone on hold says a lot. Don't look at it as a punishment, it's not. Placing someone on hold means you are taking time for yourself and will not be rushed into catering to that person's needs. It also sets the tone in the relationship early on. If you are the type who panics when you don't hear from your commitment phobe, then you'll understand what I am talking about.

How many times have you lost your cool because they ultimately took too long to text or call? Don't you know that your commit-a-phobe has you on hold? Well, they do, it's their way of not losing their own cool or getting hurt, take notes. Apologizing for outbursts to something your commit-a-phobe does only says who's really in control, they are. You are not going to have the relationship you want by doing everything right. In fact, you are making yourself sick to look at. I know you have fallen into a holding pattern, I should say, of acting this way. Now is the time to stop this chasing behavior once and for all. Look at it this way: Your commit-a-phobe is neither concerned nor worried about losing you. Why are you worrying? They are happily living their lives while you do all of the worrying, now do you see what I am talking about?

You have played this game long enough; it's causing you emotional stress. Give yourself a time-out and know that you are worth having. If you don't realize that, no one else will, not even your commit-a-phobe. It's not that your commitment phobe does not care, they do. They are not into putting themselves out to get hurt. You have to behave similarly if you want things to go your way. Giving your heart easily does not convince your commit-a-phobe that you care; it sends them in the opposite direction.

- Below is a list of ways whereby you can place your commitment phobe on hold.
- Don't make yourself available all the time.
- Say no sometimes, it helps the relationship to grow, believe it or not.
- Don't expect anything after a date, it says you are in need of attention.
- Be willing to make other plans at the last minute.
- Text your commitment phobe later rather than sooner. It tells them you are not sitting by your phone waiting for them.
- Don't accept every date they ask you out on. You must make them want to be with you. Giving anyone what they want makes you easy.
- If they call, let it ring. Finish watching television or cleaning, they can wait.
- Know you are worth the wait.

If your commit-a-phobe wants to spend time with you, they will call or text back. Saying you have other things to do does not hurt your relationship, it tells them that life does not revolve around them. You are not here to cater to them, you want that in return, so you must not be the one giving too much away. Someone who does not do well with relationships should never be chased. The last thing you want to do is send the wrong message that says, "Step on my heart, it's okay."

If you don't want to question your actions and behaviors later on, don't chase a commitment phobe. If you love this person, put them on hold from time to time. Trust me when I tell you that it will make your relationship stronger. The results that follow will amaze you because you did not give in. A commitment phobe will have very little patience or trust when it comes to love, don't blow it by being clingy. I am sure you are thinking that playing hard-to-get will send the wrong message. It will not, since a commitment phobe does not think the same way as you when it comes to spending time. Time means nothing to a commitment phobe; it's your job to make them want it, plain and simple.

They are too busy trying to be the perfect date and love of your life, the game to win you over is more fun than spending the time to get to know you.

No matter how lonely you are feeling, never let your commitment phobe see that side of you. Remember that they are looking for any reason to not give their heart to you. You will prove nothing by making yourself available every time they want you. Let's just say that if anyone should be chasing, it should be them and not you. Do you want the relationship to work or not? Are you tired of chasing your commit-a-phobe for love? Are you ready to take the relationship to the next level? Your answers should be "yes," and the only way to do that is by not getting caught up in words. Your commit-a-phobe has to prove him- or herself. Never allow sex to break your focus to what is really going on, but be sure to leave a lasting mark on them, wink.

You may not get your commit-a-phobe to fall in love overnight, but you will force them to think about you in ways they have not allowed themselves to do in a long time. You must do everything contrary to your commitment phobe if you want to win at love. Everything they want, you must not want. Less is more, as I said earlier, make your commit-a-phobe miss and need you. Just know that you can't do that by being with them all the time or by giving them what they want, it's not going to happen!

CHAPTER SEVEN
STAY FOCUSED

Now that you have your relationship in sight, stay focused. Giving too much of your time and self away is not good. You are dealing with a commit-a-phobe, which means they are not easy to love. Once more, you have put the brakes on spending time with them and focused more on yourself, wonderful! Never walk around unsure about your relationship, or you will not have one. This is just the process you must go through when dealing with a commitment phobe. Less is always more, and you must keep yourself working on your next move. By now, you know that loving a commit-a-phobe is hard work and not for the faint of heart. About now, you should be seeing progress in your relationship if you are following everything that I have been saying.

No one knows your commitment phobe and what he/she is afraid more than you, own that. Some commit-a-phobes love distraction and use it to buffer their closeness with you. Don't be taken off guard by something your commitment phobe says or does, it's how they relate to not falling for you as much as you have for them. Be prepared to feel as if you are playing a game of hide and seek, which simply means that you chase them. Chasing a commit-a-phobe is off limits and for a good reason, since it puts them in a mold of not trusting you.

Below is a list of things to keep you busy while you learn the language of your commitment phobe.

- Take up a hobby that only you love.
- Spend time with others, without them.
- Don't be so quick to check up on your commitment phobe, it's a sign of weakness or signals that you may be giving in.
- Maintain a level of control.
- Be positive in your actions.
- Think before you speak.
- Make enough time without overextending yourself.
- Be prepared to leave early, routine is not a

good idea at this stage.

In a normal relationship where the individual does not have commitment issues, you can expect things to be different. Spending time is important and a must when you are in a relationship with someone who understands the process. The rules, however, change when you have a commitment phobe. What's normal is extreme for your partner-to-be, take notice of it fast. I get it, you love being around them, but they are not seeing what you are seeing, you must fit into their world, plain and simple. If you want this relationship to work, be prepared to use patience, which will likely drive the relationship most if not all of the time.

Don't think for one moment that your commit-a-phobe has a problem with being alone, they don't. Let's just say they have managed to ruin whatever opportunity for love in their life arising over the past few years, that makes them a pro. It's as if you are dealing with the yin and yang of your relationship in the form of a person. You seek positive feelings and emotions when you are around them, they feel pressure. The pressure they feel is based on how much of themselves they feel they have to give, or trust. The goal is to be in a relationship where you both get what you want and need without pressure or fear. A take charge type of attitude is not always good in a relationship, especially for commitment phobes.

Loving a commitment phobe is hard work, and will take you staying true to yourself. It will also take you changing the way you think and view love and relationships, since it's the opposite of what your commit-a-phobe sees. Can you get married to this person and live happily ever after? Of course, you can; but as I say, it's learning about them and treating them the way they want to be treated, which is something you will have to find out.

A commitment phobe is not going to tell you how to win them over, their job is to win you over if you haven't noticed.

Below is a list of what a commitment phobe will not tell you in order to make the relationship work.

- How to get them to trust you.

- How to truly love them.
- What turns them off or on.
- What they are afraid of in the relationship.
- What you can do to assure them that you are real.
- Not to make them priority.

It's your job to find out these things on your own without their help. Once you have taken the time to know what you will not hear, you can learn what not to do. Following a commitment phobe's lead only sends the relationship down a dead end. Honesty is not their strong suit, so you should not expect them to tell you what's wrong. They can go from all-into-you to not-into-you in a matter of minutes, hours, days or weeks. Pay close attention to what a commitment phobe tells you about him- or herself and how they plan to be your everything.

Know what you are dealing with so that you will have a better chance of winning them over before they win you. The key is getting them to feel the way they want you to feel, as if they are the one. Show that you are into them, and chasing you is done. They will watch you chase them time and time again, while never giving you what you want, their love. Keep your love for them on a short leash so that you control what is going on, which in return controls the relationship. The longer you keep them in a relationship with you, the more involved and invested they become.

Keynote: Commitment phobes love to get in and out of a relationship in as little time as possible, two to three months tops. The longer you keep yourself involved with them, the more they are allowing their feelings and emotions for you to come in. This is the time when you will experience a malfunction in their ability to keep it together while looking for an escape route and calling it quits. This is not the place a commit-a-phobe wants to be, they've stayed too long with one person. Finding out the longest relationship they have ever been in is to your advantage, as it gives you a target point. When someone is giving very little of their time by making themselves the right one for you, you get caught up in the emotions and drama associated with the smoke and mirrors.

The longer you stay in your commitment phobe's life, the more they will not want to see themselves without you. You must win them over without playing games, but by having a hands-off approach, using the "less is more" rule and staying focused while also standing your ground. You become a force they can't control, and becoming your everything takes longer than expected. They love loving you and leaving you an emotional wreck, which I am sure you know already. The longer you hold out with making them the one, the longer they will chase you and not the other way around. *With that said, commitment phobes love a good game of chase, so let the chase – or, as they say, the games – begin!*

CHAPTER EIGHT
DISTRACTIONS

You are going to hit a few bumps in the road now that you have decided to move forward in your relationship. Your commit-a-phobe will try to get you off focus and more into your head. Look for your relationship to have its highs and lows in terms of emotional flare-ups. Your commitment phobe wants more of your time and attention, and may feel that you are not into them like they are with you. They are simply tired of chasing you, and it shows in their actions. You will feel as if you have bumped your head against a wall and your hard work was in vain, it was not. This is another little nasty side your commitment phobe likes to show when things are not going his/her way. They want the relationship to be over so they can stop caring or, better yet, not become attached to you.

Don't let this distract you from what you are about to do. Everything you have been working on is getting you closer to what you want. Giving in to their temper tantrum is their way of gaining some form of control. They are feeling the pressure, believe it or not. What do they do? How can they end this? How can they make it stop? This is what your emotionally wrecked commit-a-phobe is going through, taking this ride is part of the plan. If you are having a disagreement that seems to have just happened out of the blue, it's not real. If, all of a sudden, they claim you have not been giving them the attention they craved from you, it's not real. Keep in mind, your commitment phobe will turn the tables on you for not giving in to them. Sad to say, this is the only chance they have to make you feel bad. Listen to what they have to say, but never apologize for being you. Remember they felt that they were everything you were looking for and then some; if not in their words, then in their actions and behaviors.

This is the time to be clueless as to what it is they are talking about. Crying or emotional outbursts may happen for no reason at all, don't break down.

Never give in to what is happening, yet show concern without pity or the need to apologize for being you. It just so happened that you played their role better than they did, and now they have feelings they did not expect. Let your commit-a-phobe express how he/she is feeling without interrupting them. You made them fall in love with you, great job, now is not the time to blow it. They are looking for any and every reason to call you a few choice words I would rather not say here, but they earned it. Love is dangerous if you are not careful, and can have you falling in love when you least expect it. At this stage, it's clear who's driving the relationship, and it's not your commitment phobe, now is it?

Breathe and take it all in. Wipe that silly smile off your face, you still must stay focused. Help them to own their feelings by assuring them that there's nothing wrong with the way they feel about you. This will blow their minds. Not only are you in control while they are a hot mess, but you are also understanding, and you are there for them. If the commitment phobe must be angry about something, let it be his/her role in all of this, and not you feeling as if you made a fool of yourself. Be on guard for sharing and caring in the sense that your commitment phobe would want to hear how much you care or feel the same as they do. You can skim lightly on the subject without diving deep head first into a set-up. A little positive feedback is good for anyone including that commitment phobe in your life. What you say and how you say it going forward is their shifty way of gaining control of the wheel in the relationship, so be prepared to break away if you must.

Below is a list of distractions that you may get hit with when you least expect it.

- Crying out for attention.
- Shouting.
- Emotional outbursts.
- A need to know your feelings or what you think about them.
- Confirmation you care or are in love.
- A need to know that they are the only one you are seeing or love.

- You may get blasted for not caring enough.
- Not showing them enough attention.
- Not sharing your feelings or what's on your mind.
- Not falling for the bullshit they told you earlier at the get-to-know-you stage.
- Not making enough time for them.

Put on the brakes if you recognize yourself while hearing or going through the above list. Caution ahead, getting inside your head and heart is on the commitment phobe's priority list. You have not given yourself over one hundred percent in the way that leaves you vulnerable, and they know it. Getting you into a cussing and confession match is a distraction of the highest level, don't fall for it. If you don't know much about reverse psychology, now is your time to learn. Another thing to watch out for when your commitment phobe is having an emotional breakdown is what I like to call malfunction. They are not in tune to you at this moment, they need answers in any way they can get them.

Don't lose your head over what is going on or get caught up in the hype of their breakdown, which comes with a need for attention and reassurance. It will leave you wondering what may happen unless you are careful. So what do you do in this situation? I am sure you want to know.

Below is a short list of how to handle your out of control commit-a-phobe.

Look them in the eyes and say to them everything they say to you. It may sound crazy, but it works. You must mimic them and match their words and response.

Answer their questions with their own answers. If they start off saying that they have strong feelings for you and must know how you feel, your reply should be the same. This is how it looks: "I have strong feelings for you," that's it.

- Look at them and never allow them to get you angry.
- Respond not in anger but with a similar answer they may have given you.
- Never tell them or allow them to know how

much you noticed what they have been doing or not doing.
- Act clueless to what it is that they are saying. For all you know, things were good on your end. If they felt that things had been moving a little too fast, agree.
- Never be caught with more emotion or feelings than they have, it will possibly contradict your actions.

Sounding like your commit-a-phobe is not something they are expecting to hear from you. It throws them off track and out of sync with you and their emotions. Agreeing with them no matter what shows them that you are more like them than not. As I said before, commitment phobes have real issues when it comes to relationships and how they express themselves, use it against them. You will either love them or not want to have anything to do with them, but what will not happen is your heart breaking. When it comes to expressing oneself in a relationship, this is where you shine and where your commitment phobe falls apart. Allow them to fall apart without helping them in their feelings and emotions. As long as you are matching their feelings when asked, while staying true to yourself, you are handling your commit-a-phobe.

CHAPTER NINE
YOU MAKE THE RULES

In my first Sabotage book, you were told that you must realize when it's over. Now I tell you to make the rules. If you plan on taking the relationship to a much higher level, you must set the rules while understanding your commit-a-phobe. Threats of them leaving or not loving you the way that you love them should be a thing of the past. It's harder to love someone when you are not sure if you understand them. This is the case when you find yourself involved with a commitment phobe. The tables have turned, and so should you if you plan on having a lasting relationship. Should you stay, should you go, should you give them what they want every time they ask you? There are rules. There is nothing wrong with spoiling that special person in your life if they understand what is happening and why.

You are not in a position to force a normal way of

thinking onto your commit-a-phobe. Have you not been listening? Haven't you heard why they told you that they have not dated very many people for long? Weren't you listening when they told you directly that they have issues when it comes to relationships? So why on Earth are you trying to turn a plum into an apple? You are not going to get apple juice from a plum, or should I say lemon? This just says that someone isn't paying attention to the type of person they have in their life. Setting the rules only works if you know why there are rules in the first place. If you are not sure or don't have a clue, then you are playing with fire. Setting rules in a relationship that can potentially break your heart is done with a change in one's way of thinking. That means you have given up on the idea of this being a normal type of relationship, since your partner is anything but normal.

You have to become the things that you are doing or saying. Acting them out is a start, but you must become them sooner or later if you want to survive this type of relationship. What does all of that mean,

Johanna? It simply means that you have now become like a commitment phobe, but without the emotional or fearful flare-ups one may experience. Your mind has come to understand it, and you have learned how to communicate – or, as I say, speak the language of commitment phobes, if ever there is such a thing. You are like them but without the fear. You are like them without the need to run and hide. You are like them without feeling the pressure to love and leave'em. You get it, and you know how to make your commit-a-phobe feel safe instead of on edge with you. They trust you as if to trust themselves, and you have been granted access into their world. You don't expect much from them, but you understand their level of loving you. Not spending enough time does not dictate the depth of your relationship on any level.

Settling into your new position is a welcome surprise for your commit-a-phobe. You can handle them like no other. Let's not forget that you are not clingy, something they hate but love to talk about. Mixed messages are now your second language, and you speak it well. You guard your heart as well as theirs, leaving them less confused or misunderstood whenever you are around them. You are their best friend, lover and partner, something they never said, but you get it. You take everything they say with a grain of salt, *with a "don't care" attitude for lesser arguments that lead one to be misunderstood, you rock!* How can you not love them and their goofy and awkward way of letting you in?

This is what I mean by setting the rules. Everything about you becomes real, including your emotions and feelings. Spending time or seeing them doesn't decide whether you are in a relationship with them or not; you are there when they need you, and that's all that matters. Hopefully, you understand what it is that I am saying to you right about now. So what, they have not called you in a few days, that's them. So what, you have not had sex in a week, that's them. You allow them to have their time away from you without feeling the need to bother them, this is what I am getting at. Your new understanding and way of communicating speaks volumes to a commitment phobe in that you understand them like no other. It also shows a level of confidence. Many who don't understand commitment phobes seek to change them and get them out of their system. This is not what you are trying to do. You accept them for what they are, and in that they accept you for being you, which means that you have learned how to become like them in order to love them.

A commitment phobe has a certain way they need to be loved. If you understand how it works, you can love them and find that they are no different than anyone else.

CHAPTER TEN
LET THEM CHASE YOU

Nothing says "I love you" to a commitment phobe like the chase game. The more they seek after your attention, the stronger they begin to feel. Why should you let them chase you? It sets the tone for the relationship and allows them to be in control. Controlling your feelings and emotions is what they want the most, don't give in. Allow your commit-a-phobe to control other aspects of the relationship, like wanting to see you or seeking intimacy. But don't be fooled into thinking you must let them have their way every time. Your goal is to give a little bit of yourself to them over time. This means no heavy conversations about love or marriage. It also means no talking about needing or missing them, it goes to a commit-a-phobe's head.

You know what's going on, but you want to give so much more of yourself to this person who may not be able to handle it. Look at it this way: You give in, the relationship ends. Need I say more? A commitment phobe hates spending too much time, it's as if they are on a timer and must exit before it goes off, or they will be caught in loving you. If you have kept a commitment phobe in and out of your life for some time now, you've done more than most. Why can't they give in to their feelings? Why won't they trust you? These are among the questions many people ask me when dealing with the confusion of a commitment phobe. They don't understand them. Worse, they begin to not trust themselves or blame themselves for what's going on in the relationship. First, I must tell you that it's not your fault. Many times, we can't help who we fall in love with. This is why knowing how to handle a commit-a-phobe is so important to avoid going crazy.

Commitment phobes love to train the person that they are interested in, wanting more of them. This is why they make the perfect companion, if you haven't noticed. If you are not in a position to protect yourself in a relationship with a commitment phobe, you should walk away. What I should say is that the more you reach for them or ask for time, the worse they become at not giving you what you want. As you can see, a commitment phobe loves turning the tables, which keeps you guessing about what's going on in their heads. This is why I say, let them chase you, since you seem to have their attention and loyalty at that stage. Something happens to them when you give in and start to trust every word that comes out of their mouth. You are in control of what happens to you in any relationship, including with a commitment phobe. Did you know that many, if not most, commitment phobes love it when you don't give in to the bullshit they tell you? Let that sink in for just a moment before you say a word.

So why are you giving in to the bullshit and promises they are telling you? Better yet, why aren't you suspicious about the picture or image they paint of themselves? A commitment phobe, if pushed into a corner, will tell you they have issues; you just have to listen to what they are saying. Stop thinking that you can save this person from themselves or make them out to become a believer in love. Your good attitude and understanding ways do not impress them, they've seen this before. If you are really into this person, make sure it's for all of the right reasons and not you feeling you can change their minds. If you get caught up into doing this, you will be in for a world of hurt and games. I am not sure you are willing to risk your heart in order to help someone regain their trust in love.

Now that I have gotten that out of the way, letting a commit-a-phobe chase you is not bad, it's to be expected. How many people lied to them and played with their heart? How many acted the way you are acting today? So why on Earth should they trust you? For all a commit-a-phobe knows, you are trying to win them over the same way, but only to hurt them. This is the time you need to take a step back in the relationship and let things play themselves out. Keeping your head on your shoulders is where you need to be in order to take control of your emotions. Allow your commit-a-phobe to come to you by proving to you that they are serious about the next step in the relationship. Don't take anything for granted because you feel you know what's going on. A commitment phobe can easily go from hot to cold emotionally, unless you are paying close attention.

Why would you want to chase a commitment phobe, anyway? They are not the best when it comes to expressing their feelings, if you haven't noticed. Don't get caught up in proving yourself to anyone. Once you start down that road, it's hard to do anything different, and you will find yourself accepting anything when it comes to love. You desire the best in everything, and that is what you must tell yourself time and time again when dealing with a commitment phobe. Making you feel as if you don't deserve love is what they are good at. Having you believe it's your fault that the relationship is not working is another part of their game.

If you are not looking for a battle when it comes to love, I suggest that you end your relationship with a commitment phobe and be on your way. They are hard people to love because they are guarded in their feelings and with their heart. Can a relationship with a commitment phobe be positive? Yes it can, even ending in marriage, but how much are you willing to take? Letting a commitment phobe chase you in the relationship gives them the control they are looking for instead of your heart. You must be in control of your heart and feelings, as I have said time and time again, or it won't work. Less is more, and standing your ground sets the stage for what's to come in the next phase of your relationship.

Can I Help Them Let Go Of Their Fears?

This was shared in Sabotage One, and I felt that it must be added in order for you to understand what's at stake. How can I deal with this one? It seems everyone I know wants to save the world one man or woman at a time, but let me be the first to tell you that you can't help everyone you date to think or act like you, especially if they are not asking for your help. If you see that the person you are dating has commitment issues that are getting in the way of the relationship growing, it's time for you to step away before you become brokenhearted.

I am sure you love or have grown very close to the person you are dating or have married. You can't make them let go of their fears and pain of past issues, it's their job to let go. You can't make them want to talk about what hurts them with you, it will never happen. A commitment phobe's thought process is different from yours and mine. They are protecting themselves first, and the truth of who and what they are is never shared. You are just allowing yourself to be a victim, for the sake of what? If a commitment phobe wants to talk, they will let you know after they break your heart, when they say goodbye.

How can you help someone if you can't see you are being played by a commitment phobe? Helping a person with commitment phobias can be stressful in some cases, especially when you know that this person is resistant to you due to them not wanting to be in a long-term relationship. I have friends that have gone through this process who were used, and who thought they could save the person they were dating from themselves, teaching them how to love. It did not happen, and the other person ended the relationship for fear of being forced to love. What many people don't know is that commitment phobes don't want to learn anything from you since they are not interested in giving themselves to you or being truthful about anything. Once they start lying to you, they simply can't stop.

They have sized you up well before talking to you,

knowing from their past experiences where you fall on the hurt scale. They know what they can do to you to cause hurt, that's why you have to get them before they get you. Staying in such a dysfunctional relationship is damaging to you, so get out today or you will end up fighting them to love and care about you. You must learn how to handle your commit-a-phobe if you want it to work.

What you really need to know is that at the end of the day, everyone has been hurt by a lover or two, but when you are purposely going around wounding others for the sake of doing so, you are only hurting yourself. Nothing is accomplished when a commitment phobe acts this way, you see them suffer because of low self-esteem. Now is not the moment to be asking questions, but to give them the time they need to process what's happening to them.

If you are able to see the signs early in a commitment phobe, know that staying in a relationship where you are loved to death in the sense of lies, betrayal and deceit is not going to make them or you better, it will make matters worse. Be true to yourself and your feelings without giving too much of your heart away.

Why do we feel the need to save a commitment phobe? What relationship in your past needed saving? Stop dealing with the past and get on with your life. Haven't you been through enough? When you are involved with someone who has relationship issues, it's like dealing with a broken person who has never healed. One minute they are in, and the next minute they are out. They never know what they want from day to day, people feel this way when married to a commitment phobe. There are times when you may see your spouse wanting to save the marriage and times when they don't give a damn. Most commitment phobes are not looking for anyone at their level, they are not looking to be told what to do and how to do it by someone who knows what they want. They are constantly thinking of ways to get the relationship over with. You must not allow that to happen.

Below are signs you need to look for when dealing with a difficult relationship.

- A commitment phobe loves telling negative stories about their past relationships. Lying is at the top of their list.

- A commitment phobe is always cautious and untrusting of others, including you. They are always up to no good, and are looking for the next relationship to jump into once they are done having fun with you. This is not where you want to be.

- A commitment phobe always needs some type of assurance from you that they are doing the right thing, like making you happy. Most commitment phobes suffer with their sexual self-image.

- A commitment phobe never likes to take accountability for issues in the relationship since they are looking to exit at the drop of a hat. Most start looking for the next person to date while dating you or being married to you. This is not the time to become sensitive.

- Most commitment phobes love to play the victim for getting attention from you and others around you. They are always hurting, and someone has always done something to them to make them feel the way they do. *Big crybabies!*

- A commitment phobe is not in touch with their feelings and those of their partner, you will never hear them say sorry for anything they say or do that ends up hurting you. Once they have pushed you to the end is when they say sorry. Their expression of regret is not genuine. *This is why you must speak their language.*

- A commitment phobe loves to keep watch over how much you spend, but will never allow you to say anything about what they do with their money. They are control freaks.

- A commitment phobe may be confident one minute and insecure the next. These mood swings are enough to drive one crazy, especially if they happen frequently. *I guess you need to have a few mood swings.*

- A commitment phobe may feel the need to tell you what you can and cannot do, but you are not allowed to tell them anything since they have things under control. They so want to be the Boss!

- A commitment phobe will get an attitude with you quickly since they don't like to be told what to do by anyone. They do as they please. *And so should you!*
- A commitment phobe loves to rush others, but not to be rushed. It's a double standard.
- A commitment phobe loves to give someone the silent treatment in a relationship when things don't go their way. *Learn the silent treatment!*
- A commitment phobe will punish you by not talking to you or by staying out late, not calling you or texting you when you don't cater to their feelings and their every need.
- A commitment phobe is good at promising you the world, and seems to have all of the qualities you want after the first date, yet they never deliver on anything they offer you. *Don't believe the hype!*
- A Commitment phobe will push back from a relationship they feel is moving towards a long-term relationship, a commitment phobe

will start complaining about problems with you that you never knew they had. *All smoke and mirrors!*

- When a commitment phobe is meeting new people around you, they will mention negative things about you behind your back. This is to set the stage early on in the relationship for them to make their grand exit out of the relationship, since it gives them a good alibi.

- A commitment phobe is a good salesperson, who can talk to you about marriage and you being the one. The truth comes when they never want to agree on or set a date, and any proposed dates they discuss with you are often allowed to pass with no mention of them. Kind of slick when you think about it.

- A commitment phobe knows they are full of shit; they need to convince others of their feelings for you even if they are lies since the more believers they have, the more truthful it sounds.

- A commitment phobe will suddenly take time alone by using family and friends to get away from you. This is a sign the relationship is coming to an end, and they just have to find the exit door before you see it.

- A commitment phobe wants approval from someone even if that happens to be your family and friends.
- As you can see, this list can go on and on since there is no set of rules when dealing with someone who can't commit to you.

Now that you are stuck in a relationship where you start to long for the commitment phobe's attention and time, they refuse to give you what you want.

You can't make someone do something they are unwilling to do, and this is true when dealing with a commitment phobe. Most commitment phobes' relationships are built on disappointment, bitterness and lies, which is how they see the relationship.

CHAPTER ELEVEN
MORE RED FLAGS

You can't get around the truth even when it's staring you in the face. Commitment phobes send red flags that must not be ignored. If you choose not to see what's going on, it will cost you later on. The only way to handle a commitment phobe is to understand the red flags. You must know when they want to be alone without them asking you to step back. You must know when your behavior or attention is getting on their nerves. Below is a list of red flags you must watch for.

- Not texting you back or calling you right away.
- Not wanting to spend time with you.
- Changing their plans, which ends up leaving you out.
- Not being truthful about their feelings.
- Making you feel as if they don't care.
- Having a "don't care" attitude to your

feelings.
- Not being willing to share their feelings about anything.
- Becoming silent and secretive.
- Have a change in their behavior or mood.
- Not making sense when you talk to them.
- Having a lack of attention or communication on their part.

Keeping you in the dark many times is their way of needing time away from what's going on. Some commitment phobes have no problems letting you know they are afraid of trusting anyone. The more you push them to give in to you, the more they will reject you. Speaking the language of a commitment phobe is not hard, and you should know that before you allow your feelings to rule. A commitment phobe just wants to be loved no different than anyone else, but on their terms and with their conditions. You can't force someone to love and trust you. Showing someone how you feel and teaching them how to treat you is the only way to build any type of trust.

Don't think for one minute that a commitment phobe is not watching your every move, they are. Social media is one way they get to know you. Learning what makes your commit-a-phobe run and hide is key to making the relationship work. Grow tough skin if you aren't planning on letting them go. As you know, a commit-a-phobe will push you until you break. The goal is to get in and out of the relationship with their heart and emotions intact.

Now is the time to set boundaries in the relationship that protect your heart. Below is a list of ways to guard your heart with a commit-a-phobe.

- Lose the fear of losing them.
- Keep busy.
- Don't make a commit-a-phobe the primary person in your life.
- Learn to have a level of comfort with them, a sort of take-it-or- leave-it attitude.
- Keep your feelings and emotions out of the way.

At times, sharing your feelings is what you will want to do. I caution you to keep them to yourself as you get to know your commit-a-phobe. In time, you will be able to say the things that you want without feeling as if your emotions and feelings have been hijacked. Everything you are thinking, so too is your commit-a-phobe. They don't feel safe until you can't live without them; crazy as that sounds, it's true. If you are not looking to hand over your heart on a silver platter, learn to speak and think like a commitment phobe.

When a commitment phobe starts feeling the need to exit the relationship, they try to do so without you knowing. Face it, they need an easy way out, and your constant nagging is just what they are looking for.

Once they feel they have you where they want you, a commitment phobe will no longer want you around. They will pull back their love from you quickly. So know the red flags, so that you give them the time and distance they need without experiencing the fear of losing them.

CHAPTER TWELVE
REALIZING IT'S OVER

I could not move on without covering this chapter once again. Although you hate to think about it, sometimes it's better to say goodbye instead of trying to make it work. And now you finally have come to the end of your rope with this relationship, now you are ready to give it up because you're drained from trying to work it out. Really, you should not be surprised by the realization that your relationship is ending, since you have been on this road with a commitment phobe for some time now. Now that you are ready to walk away, they are the ones fighting for the relationship to work, but you have been down this road so many times that you have lost count. What have you learned? Why should you stay? These are the questions that are stuck in your mind. Can I do this again? Is it worth it? The true answer is within you, that is what you should be listening to.

A commitment phobe will wait until the

relationship is so stressed out that it lies flat before jumping back in to save it one last time, but this is done to make them feel good about themselves instead of feeling like a failure. They know what you can and cannot take, and love to see you in this mental state; most would say it's cruel seeing you this way. Not every relationship with a commitment phobe ends in days, weeks or months. Some last for years, believe it or not, and the person who wants everything to work out ends up struggling alone in the relationship. No matter how much progress you make with a commitment phobe, they will always reset themselves back to what they feel is their truth, which ends up with them not committing to you. *In order to handle your commit-a-phobe, you must allow them to have this truth they hold onto, which is hurt and pain.*

Many times, a commitment phobe will not allow themselves to be burdened by such feelings of love and commitment because they know they were never really going to stay. But they play a very strong role as if they are affected when clearly they are not. I know many people who went through this, only to come to the understanding that they had to move on with their lives. This happened when they realized that the "loving person" they were with was more like a death or cancer in their life rather than something good.

When dealing with someone who has not truly experienced love, teaching them how to love seems easy enough. When you are dealing with a commitment phobe, love is not an option since they are fearful of it. It's like you are dealing with their past, which they are unable to let go of. You will never change that fact; you believe that you can love another person so much that they will stop hurting. That way of thinking is what keeps you holding on and being fooled. No one can bring someone past their hurt and pain, it is up to that person to let go and move on. The only role you will end up playing with a commitment phobe is the one they allow you to play in their life; and from where I am sitting, it's more like a hit and run.

When you realize you can't change someone's

way of thinking about love and commitment, you will stop lying to yourself and allowing that person to love you to death by making you unhappy and miserable. You may be hurt now that you are giving up on the relationship, or maybe you feel like you are giving up too soon, but ask yourself this: Aren't you tired? Why are you the only one fighting for this relationship to work? Your freedom to pursue the life and type of relationship you want is on the other side of this relationship once you let go.

So realizing that you've gone through a lot in such a short period of time, all the love and emotions you felt for this person are now overshadowed by disgust and anger. Don't let these feelings make you become the next commitment phobe in a relationship. Forgive yourself for staying and putting up with all of the things you did, and move on without any regrets.

Your happiness is based on your ability to forgive yourself for staying with a broken person; from that, you can move on to bigger and better things. Once you let go, keep that door closed by not allowing that person to run in and out of your life, that is how you start the healing process. You should never be afraid to search for love, but know that it's love you are attracting to you and nothing else. On the other side of your hurt and pain is the relationship you have been looking for. Now is the time to go to it, just make sure you leave behind your past hurts, anger and mixed emotions with the commitment phobe.

Many people say that when things don't go your way in life, smile and move on. When you do this, you will see that you'll be better off alone than stuck with someone who is holding onto life situations like it were a life jacket.

In their case, the life jacket doesn't work and becomes more like a death jacket or a death trap; they are going down fast, and you were entangled in their web before you broke free. Now you see yourself as free-falling towards something so much better for you; smile, you are on your way! Walking away does not mean you failed at love. Don't associate a failed relationship with your ability to love someone outside of yourself. You did not have a problem with loving someone; unfortunately, the person you chose to be in your life did. That person will miss out on a wonderful, loving and caring person to share their life with, but that's no longer your concern.

You will feel sick and out of sorts for a while, but as soon as you get back to living, life will open up for you with a wonderful surprise. No matter who they move on to next, it will never be real since they are so imprisoned by hurt and pain. *Don't let this bad relationship experience make you the next saboteur!*

Don't Get Abused

In your process to find love with a commitment phobe, don't get abused or settle for their way of loving you. Have you ever noticed that when things do not go the way the commitment phobe in your life wants, they can be very abusive? In fact, they will blame you for everything that goes wrong in the relationship; and if you are not careful, you could end up believing it. If you are not the reason for their feelings, I am sure they will look back far enough into their past to find something that does the trick. Can you see how this type of person is harmful to your life? Can you see how they can cause you so much damage that you stop loving and trusting others? It's a wonder you have not lost your mind in all of the relationships you've had with commitment phobes.

I've learned that broken relationships lead to broken hearts, and those hearts end up hurting others they come into contact with if the person is not very careful. What type of abuse are you dealing with in your relationship? Has the other person said they were sorry a dozen times, only to do it again? One of my family members was involved with someone who was more into hurting them than being truthful about their feelings. They fought and did things to hurt each other time and time again. It was the only way this person could deflect from what they were doing without being obvious. The real reason why commitment phobes become abusive in their relationship has nothing to do with you, but more to do with them feeling the need to protect themselves from love, commitment and getting hurt. Now, where does that leave you?

No one should stay in any relationship that hurts them mentally or physically. Loving someone should not feel like a battle. Thinking about what you want out of your relationship if you are with a commitment phobe is the best way of taking the necessary steps towards walking away. I would never tell someone to walk away from their relationship, but if you are dealing with a commitment phobe and things are not getting any better, you may have to leave.

The sad truth is that many people never make it out of these types of relationships, and end up scarred for life. The longer you stay with a commitment phobe who does not want to commit to you, the more you risk becoming just like them. Don't live your life in a relationship where you become broken pieces of the person you once were. You become the scapegoat in the relationship. Can you say: I had nothing to do with their childhood or last relationship issues? Can you also say: I am not the person who abandoned them in life? You are not responsible for the bad things that happen in their life, don't you ever accept that.

You will never know what baggage someone is carrying around until they allow you to get close enough to see; and by this time, you have already seen more than you wanted to. This is why I also say it would be nice to see packaging information on the forehead of someone you are thinking about dating. What would appear on the forehead could be, "Approach with caution! This individual may have the tendencies to isolate you, blame you or become critical of you, threaten you, the more you get to know them." Since this is not the case, you have to be aware of the actions and behaviors of the person you are dating or interested in, then hold them and not yourself accountable for what happens.

Every second of the day, someone you know may be dealing with a commitment phobe while being too ashamed to say anything about it. You never have to feel shame in order to experience love. You must not become angry, bitter, heartbroken, disrespected or humiliated for someone to truly love you. You also don't have to stay in a relationship that does not value you as a person and that keeps you emotionally broken and confused from day to day. Below are a few signs and tricks used by those who seek to turn you into a victim.

- Demeaning – You feel humiliated as your character is attacked. You try to speak up for yourself in the relationship, only to be put down and ignored.
- Gas lighting – You are given false information by the commitment phobe, while your abuse claims about the relationship are denied, making you look like you are going crazy, out of your mind.
- Isolation – You are made to feel guilty for spending time with family and friends. You are also made to feel guilty for doing anything that you love and that keeps you happy. A commitment phobe loves to

control others.

- Criticizing – You feel as if you never do anything right in their eyes, and are put down by their words. Your shortcomings are the highlights of the conversation more than anything else.
- Blaming – You are never right about anything, you are made to feel as if everything is your fault when you know it's not. A feeling of helplessness takes root.
- Threatened – You never feel safe in your own relationship, and live life on eggshells for fear of losing the one and only person you love, who doesn't love or give a damn about you.
- The Silent Treatment – You are ignored when you do speak up. It's enough to stop you from talking, mission completed. If you feel as if you are being punished for speaking your mind, then you are.

It's never easy staying in a relationship with someone who promised you the moon and stars, yet you're still waiting on that delivery. Face it, you are with a commitment phobe who has issues, which is not your fault. So why are you punishing yourself for someone else's way of thinking? Stop allowing yourself to be victimized while waiting for love to show up at your door. Below are a few positive keys you can use to take control of your life and get your emotions back on track.

- Know who you are dealing with – A commitment phobe will come across as sweet, loving and understanding; but deep down, they are far from it, they are really just a copycat of something they used to be before they got hurt.
- Trust yourself – Don't look to someone else's truth as your own, nor accept their promises as a good faith justification for putting up with hell. Answer to your heart and step away. Even when you don't want to acknowledge that something is wrong, your inner soul has already given you the answers, will you listen? Trusting yourself is

the first sign of self-love.

- Forgive yourself – The second sign of loving yourself is to forgive your mistakes, just as you would others'. Pay attention to this moment in your life because it has brought you to the point you're at today. We all make mistakes from time to time, but forgiving yourself is the only way you can move on to a better you. You can't save everyone and risk losing yourself in the process.
- Break free – It's never easy giving up on someone you had invested in, but when love hurts and burns, it's time to jump up and move on. Loving someone is never meant to destroy or dehumanize you.
- Know your worth – See yourself as someone who is deserving of real and true love and not a counterfeit version. Loving someone is not supposed to destroy you in the process, you never should feel as if it's your responsibility to make a bad relationship

work. The only responsibility you have is to yourself and your happiness. Make sure, when it comes to relationships, that you are giving and receiving the same in return.

How long are you going to blame yourself for someone else's actions? You should know that whatever happens in your relationship is not your fault alone, it takes two to make something work and one to destroy it. Something inside of you should be tapping on your heart to move on. If you can't save yourself, try saving your heart. How long are you going to deny yourself from someone who deserves you?

How long are you going to ignore your truth? These are questions you should be asking yourself if you are in a relationship with a commitment phobe who's not valuing you but victimizing you. You should never feel alone or scared to leave a bad situation.

CHAPTER THIRTEEN
REINVENTING A NEW YOU

I could not end this without addressing a time for change. I have added a few chapters from my previous book. Reinventing a new you is not hard, but it's necessary after a breakup. Taking all that you have been through in trying to make a relationship work with someone you thought you knew, but who turned out to be a liar and a fake, is a hard pill to swallow. *You must address the fact of your relationship not working, it's up to the commitment phobe to let you into their world.*

You must know that not everyone is going to celebrate your success, not even the person you thought was the best thing that had ever happened to you, once you've found out the true nature of their games. I know you are hurting, and that smile on your face is a way to show those close to you that you are no longer affected. You suffered disgrace, hurt and lies in your relationship, and smiled your way through it around those you love.

Knowing that life is short, as one would always say, tells you that feeling sad and down about being lied to is not going to change the outcome of what took place. You simply have to pull it together and move on. Do you remember those days when you were the happiest in your life and it seemed like nothing else mattered? What about the days when you felt good about the direction you were moving in before getting involved with someone who sought to hurt and destroy your life with secrets and lies?

You have to realize that you are stronger than you know and will get past those feelings and emotions in no time. Right now, I want you to act as if you are past those emotions by not allowing yourself to relive the bad things that took place in your life.

Can you see the sunshine ahead and smell the fresh air around you? Can you picture yourself happy, in love and with the person you were meant to be with? Can you smile when everything inside of you tells you to cry? How you see through this time of transition in your life will prepare your heart for the next journey ahead. We all know that life is full of surprises; some good and some bad, especially when it comes to letting someone inside your heart, but it should never stop you from being who you are.

See yourself past this moment, and soon you will feel your heart healing even if this means that you must let go of some of the things you loved having while in that not-so-happy relationship. Many times, we try to take the past into the future, but it just does not work out the way we wanted, and that's okay. Be willing to box up some good times you had in the form of pictures and gifts given to you from a past relationship that did not work out, then move on. Below are a few things I recommend after your relationship is over.

- Have fun and live life.
- Give yourself a makeover. Nothing says it's a new day like getting one.
- Letting go of old memories is a great way to start a new life and a new you.
- Box up your past if you have to!

- Think of the next person you would like to meet. What are some qualities you would like the next person you date to have?
- Stay away from negative people who only seek to remind you of how messed up your relationship really was.
- Travel somewhere you have never been before, and take a friend or someone you trust that will keep you laughing.
- Know that you are worthy of love and will find it when you are ready.
- Decorate your place and get out of the past by adding a splash of color or scented candles that put you in a relaxed mood.

There are still so many things that you can do to help move past your hurt and start a new life, but it will have to take you wanting to move forward. Worrying about the things that made you unhappy when you felt that you were in a good place will only keep you down. Life is what you make of it, and not everyone in life has a great relationship story to tell, but know that your story is there for your growth into a better you.

Give yourself credit for getting out of a bad situation we all know was not easy; but guess what, you did it. You are the key to your own happiness, which starts with you.

Stay Away from Takers

I am sure that about now, you have a clear understanding of what a commitment phobe is after all of the chapters you have read, but don't be fooled into thinking that you have nothing to worry about as you move forward in dating and meeting new people. You still must carry a bit of caution when making friends or dating, this is the rule. Although your heart and intentions may be good, not everyone else's are, and for this reason, you have to look at everyone as a suspect until you have a clear understanding of who and what you are dealing with.

Let's say, for instance, that you have just gotten out of a bad relationship and that, knowing that the person you were dating before was a commitment phobe, you ignored the red flags and warning signs for the sake of giving someone a chance, but it did not work out. I am sure you had the gut feeling that something was not right with this person, or they were just too good to be true. Let's say that you dated them anyway, and now you are happy to be out of that worthless relationship. I am sure you have a million negative things you can say to justify your feelings and emotions, but you must know these will not keep the next commitment phobe from entering your life.

These folks are takers. A taker will never give you what you want, and unless you move away from them or learn their language, they will only follow you because they are looking for someone like you or for something that can make them happy.

The old give and take is not always true, and for a commitment phobe, take is all they know how to do, which is why they leave their victims in a relationship devastated. To ensure that your next relationship becomes one that is healthy and safe, you have to put the nice person aside when you see red flags popping up all around you. Nice people never get the person or the relationship that they really want because they are too busy being used as a doormat. *Stop being a doormat and learn how to not beg for love.*

Letting someone wipe their feet on your heart is never okay and should never be accepted as a way of getting to know someone, or worse, keeping someone in your life. I am sure you are probably thinking: Who would allow someone to do that to them? But you would be surprised what people will do to have someone in their life.

A person with commitment phobias is focused and know what they want and what they will not allow, which means that they are selfish while you are trusting. Last time I checked, those I love who were in relationships, even friendships, like this were left heartbroken. If you are a person that feels you can get anyone to love you because you have that effect on others, you need to really think again when dealing with people who have these issues. The more problems a person has, the more these will reflect in their inability to have a successful and long-lasting relationship with anyone.

We all have been around someone in our life who wants more, needs more and asks for more than they are willing to give. We see them in their everyday life and swear to ourselves that we will never date or marry such a person because we have witnessed this behavior around us. Still, we find ourselves in such relationships years later. Are you asking yourself how in the heck you got here? Why have you accepted a person who does not respect you? Why are you settling for someone who swore they would never marry you? Why are you so afraid of being alone? What is it about this person that makes you disregard everything you told yourself you would never accept or tolerate? Why are you allowing yourself to be used? *Because you want to be loved, and your commit-a-phobe knows it. Today, you will not cry over spilled milk or the need for love. You will understand who and what you are dealing with. You will also take control of the relationship, since a commitment phobe will not, and if you can't, it's time for you to exit the relationship.*

Are you willing to walk into this relationship with your eyes closed? Are you closing your eyes when the red flags pop up so that you don't have to deal with it or, better yet, make a decision? These are important questions that you should be asking yourself now that you've found yourself another commitment. Now is the time to know the signs of a taker since most people who date commitment phobes tend to draw the same type of person around them every time.

A taker is someone that wants you to prove yourself to them, but sits in judgment of you.

A taker is someone who is always right and never wants to compromise, especially if it will make them wrong.

A taker is someone who tells you what they want and doesn't care how you feel.

Takers never play by the rules of dating. Because they have been used, hurt and suffer from low self-esteem, they are only looking for a pick-me-up through hurting others like yourself.

A taker does not care about your heart or if they break it, they are more concerned about not getting hurt by anyone, so their mindset is: I will get you before you get me!

A taker is an enemy of the relationship and love.

A taker wants to prove that they are right about how they treat people because of all the wrongful things they have encountered.

A taker sees you as a prize in a game, and the game is how fast they can convince you to believe in them.

A taker sees relationships through your eyes, yet carries a destructive mentality in order to feel safe whenever they are with you.

Today, you are no longer a taker in the eyes of your commitment phobe because you hold the cards. If you are dating for looks, you are one step closer to finding a commitment phobe. Weigh out the person's heart, and don't just take their word for it. I am sure we all have that relationship resume that paints us in a favorable light when we may be far from it, having a lot of work ahead of us on how we see relationships.

The world around us is one that is built on taking; therefore, you will see more takers than givers. Now this does not mean that you will never find the person that you want, it just means that you will have to be a little more patient and understanding when dating. You also have to not be taken by smooth words and nice outings during dating because many people get caught up in the process and forget about the person they are truly dealing with. *Know the commitment phobe's ways ahead of time.*

Focus is the key to dating, not nice words, compliments or how much money someone is willing to spend on you since, in the end, it will mean nothing if the person has a taker's mindset. This is the same behavior of a commitment phobe. Whether they are male or female, they have to put in a little investing to get a quick return on those investments, such as heartfelt emotions that are believable. That quick return is your open, trusting heart that they are looking to take, along with sex, money and whatever they feel they can get from you now that you are open to them.

Have you ever been around someone that has fallen in love literally overnight, but you are trying to get them to see things clearly so that they won't get hurt, except they see you as a hater against their new relationship? After a few weeks or months, their relationship has fizzled down to nothing, and they are looking for love again, more trusting than ever before. If you have seen this happen to someone you know, then you witnessed the return of the commitment phobe.

For young women out there who are allowing themselves to get pregnant with a man simply because he said he is ready for a family but not marriage, this should be a red flag and sign that you are dealing with a commitment phobe. Who on Earth will want the responsibility of a child but not as a full-time parent? If you are allowing yourself to get pregnant for the sake of keeping your relationship intact, for the sake of someone who at the drop of a hat wants something, then you are allowing yourself to be victimized by a commitment phobe.

Do you feel that a child should have the support of both parents? Do you feel that a child should see both of their parents? This is not addressing those in relationships who have tried to make things work, then realized that it's over. These questions are for those young and some old foolish lovers who are requesting things in a dating phase with no chances of having a fully committed relationship. Maybe you have asked the question about commitment and marriage and received a yes, maybe you have asked those questions and received mixed answers. This is when you should be getting that gut feeling telling you what's really going on.

I know that gut feeling is not a popular topic for conversation because it's a big indicator that something is wrong, something you don't want to have to face or deal with. Still, we are all built with this indicator inside of us, whether we use it or not.

If you know you are dating someone who is not

good for you, and they have sent you mixed messages in the name of love, it's time to get out of that relationship unless you are willing to drive it. The longer you stay with someone who is unwilling to give you what you need, the more you lose bits and pieces of who you are, and the more you die inside. The worst part of all of this is that you leave the relationship as a commitment phobe and wind up hurting someone else.

- Stop the cycle of killing those who love you because of bad choices you've made in your past.
- Stop the cycle of dating people who are not fit to be in your life.
- Stop the cycle of giving people a chance because you believe in love.
- Stop the cycle of giving everyone the benefit of the doubt.
- Stop the cycle of killing and ruining your life because you don't want to be alone.
- Stop the cycle of lying to yourself.
- Stop the cycle of ignoring that gut feeling

that's trying to keep you safe.
- Stop the cycle of having a broken heart.
- Stop the cycle of going back to a commitment phobe.
- Stop the cycle of dating your exes, they are your exes for a reason.
- Stop the cycle of allowing people to lie to your face.
- Stop the cycle of thinking you can change how people think.
- Stop the cycle of pretending you don't see what's going on.

Just stop it! If you love yourself, your job is to protect your heart, and you can do that by not allowing yourself to tricked, fooled and lied to. Wherever you are in your life today, look at it as a time for growth, and only allow those people into your life who are capable of growing with you.

- Trust yourself.
- Love yourself.

- Be kind to yourself.
- Know that you deserve the best.
- Protect your heart from strangers.
- Learn to listen without trusting or giving away your heart.
- Keep your emotions in control.
- Don't make sex your reason for love, knowing that attraction can be seen in the heart and physical attraction can be a distraction from one's heart, if that's all you are looking for.

Follow your heart when it comes to what's right and wrong, trust your gut feeling even if that person is telling you to trust them. No one knows you like you know yourself, and that's what you have in your corner. How many times did you feel like something was wrong and you were right? How many times have you seen through someone knowing they were no damn good for you, and was proven right later on? So, why on Earth are you not trusting yourself?

If you want something good, you will know it

when it comes. If you just want something quick, you are opening up yourself and your heart to death. Love is not death, but commitment phobes are. So as long as you have those two in your rearview mirror, you are bound to steer clear of a head-on collision with your heart.

Never be that person who tells themselves, "I told you so!" So the next time you see signs of a commitment phobe heading your way, run away yelling "no thank you!" if you aren't willing to control the relationship!

TALK WITH JOHANNA SPARROW

Get Your Relationship Back on Track With Life Coach and Relationship Expert

Antoinette Watkins A.K.A Johanna Sparrow

FREE 30-Minute Phone Session for New Clients ONLY!
Skype Sessions are available

Get Your FREE eBook Download on Smashwords: "Breakthrough."

30-Minute and 1 Hour Phone Sessions are Available. Schedule today at
https://www.10minuterelationshipadvicewithjohannasparrow.com/

Also visit me at: https://www.johannasparrow.com/
email:askjohanna@johannasparrow.com

A WORD OF ADVICE FROM JOHANNA SPARROW

We all love to have someone who understands and loves us, but we do not always find what we are looking for. Love can happen whether that person accepts it and believes in it or not. The law of attraction, once set in motion, cannot be stopped, and we find ourselves lashing out at love instead of welcoming it. The best relationships are not always those where both people think alike, nope. It's the relationship where opposites attract, and I do mean attract. "How long do you hang on?" is the question for many. "When do you give in or let go?" is the question for others. A person can't truly love unless they know what it is they are loving and why. It's not enough to want someone, you have to understand them if it is going to work. What you should know is that you can't force someone to love you, they either love you or they don't.

Giving yourself to someone who does not understand you can leave a bitter taste in your mouth if you are not careful. More people are in love with the concept of having someone in their lives to call their own – a concept that has destroyed many in the name of love. Love and allowing love to come in is a battle many don't want to get involved with, but you know this already, I am sure. Let things happen the way they should. Leave your idea of what love is out of the equation when getting to know someone else. Your way of loving someone else may be wrong for them. Learn about the person before loving them, and you will have a better chance at love.

If all that person has experienced is rejection, the need to define the meaning of love may be crucial to them playing a role that fills your desire. Know that not everyone is worth the wait and that it's okay to walk away for something better, even if it hasn't shown up. Getting to a place where love is experienced on both sides is where you want to be in order for things to work. Otherwise, you are just wasting precious time. Don't be afraid to step outside of your comfort zone to know someone, you will be surprised at what life can teach you when you expect nothing in return. *When handling a commitment phobe, this is what you must live by, nothing in return!*

YOUR PERSONALIZED PRESCRIPTION FOR A COMMIT-A-PHOBE

- Respect yourself.
- Never chase them.
- Give your relationship space.
- Never text or call right away.
- Have a hobby, or something to keep you busy.
- Don't be needy or clingy.
- Have a relaxed take-it-or-leave-it type of attitude.
- Know that less is more with a commitment phobe.
- Never show fear of losing them.
- Make them chase after you.
- Don't give away your feelings.
- Don't make them your everything too soon.
- Make them prove themselves to you.
- Find out their dating history.
- Date them longer than anyone else.
- Be patient.
- Expect nothing while giving small parts of yourself.
- Never set a routine.
- Never allow them to know you or what you are thinking.

J Sparrow

ABOUT THE AUTHOR

Antoinette M Watkins writes under the pen name Johanna Sparrow. She has been writing for over 17 years, and has published a variety of books from children's books to self-help books dealing with relationships, personal growth and conflict issues. She uses her expertise, knowledge and experience on a system she's created and used over the years dating back as far as 1995 in improving relationship issues, called the (HBCCR)© Heart Bruised Conscious Connection Renewal codes, which we either have or don't have inside of us.

In 2015, Johanna Sparrow will release, for the first time, her powerful and inspiring HBCCR system she's created to the rest of the world in hopes that we all can find a common goal or ground within our daily connections.

She has researched and studied, over the years, connections between human-to-human and human-to-nature interactions in which she concluded in her research how understanding one's connections and disconnections in life is the essential step code and laws for love, happiness and tragedy, governing and guiding us in becoming life's greatest or worst creation to ever exist.

Made in the USA
Las Vegas, NV
18 July 2021